J 641.3 ROS
Rose, Simon, 1961– author.
Evaluating arguments about food

State Your Case

Evaluating Arguments About Food

Simon Rose

CRABTREE
PUBLISHING COMPANY
WWW.CRABTREEBOOKS.COM

Author: Simon Rose
Series research and development: Reagan Miller
Editors: Sarah Eason, Claudia Martin, Jennifer Sanderson, and Janine Deschenes
Proofreaders: Tracey Kelly, Wendy Scavuzzo
Indexer: Tracey Kelly
Editorial director: Kathy Middleton
Design: Paul Myerscough
Cover design: Katherine Berti
Photo research: Claudia Martin
Production coordinator and Prepress technician: Katherine Berti
Print coordinator: Katherine Berti

Produced for Crabtree Publishing Company by Calcium Creative Ltd

Photo Credits:
t=Top, c=Center, b=Bottom, l=Left, r=Right.

Inside: Scott Bauer, USDA ARS: p.30; Shutterstock: 06photo: p.32; anyaivanova: p.28; Arina P Habich: pp.3, 19; arindambanerjee: p.29; Arisara T: p.11; branislavpudar: p.5; ChameleonsEye: p.15; Denys Kurbatov: p.36; Ekaterina Markelova: p.21; Glenda: p.43; Gutesa: p.25; LADO: p.6; Lapina: p.10; lenetstan: p.38; LightField Studios: p.4; majivecka: p.22; Michelle Baumbach: p.37; miya227: p.7; Monkey Business Images: pp.9, 13, 14, 40; Ozphotoguy: p.31; plantic: p.16; Poznyakov: p.24; preechna2531: p.23; Rapax: p.18; Rawpixel.com: p.20; Reinhold Leitner: p.34; Roman Selliutin: p.42; Sean Xu: p.33; Sergey Novikov: p.39; Sharomka: pp.1, 26; SpeedKingz: p.41; Studio Peace: p.17; successo images: p.12; thka: p.35; wavebreakmedia: p.8; Yummy pic: p.27.

Cover: All images from Shutterstock

Library and Archives Canada Cataloguing in Publication

Rose, Simon, 1961-, author
   Evaluating arguments about food / Simon Rose.

(State your case)
Includes bibliographical references and index.
Issued in print and electronic formats.
ISBN 978-0-7787-5077-2 (hardcover).--
ISBN 978-0-7787-5090-1 (softcover).--
ISBN 978-1-4271-2162-2 (HTML)

   1. Food--Juvenile literature. 2. Food--Moral and ethical aspects--Juvenile literature. 3. Critical thinking--Juvenile literature. 4. Thought and thinking--Juvenile literature. 5. Reasoning--Juvenile literature. 6. Persuasion (Rhetoric)--Juvenile literature. I. Title.

TX357.R664 2018   j641.3   C2018-903029-1
                                            C2018-903030-5

Library of Congress Cataloging-in-Publication Data

CIP available at the Library of Congress

Printed in the U.S.A./092018/CG20180810

Crabtree Publishing Company
www.crabtreebooks.com   1-800-387-7650

Copyright © **2019 CRABTREE PUBLISHING COMPANY**. All rights reserved. No part of this publication may be reproduced, stored in a retrieval system, or be transmitted in any form or by any means, electronic, mechanical, photocopying, recording, or otherwise, without the prior written permission of Crabtree Publishing Company. In Canada: We acknowledge the financial support of the Government of Canada through the Canada Book Fund for our publishing activities.

Published in Canada
Crabtree Publishing
616 Welland Ave.
St. Catharines, Ontario
L2M 5V6

Published in the United States
Crabtree Publishing
PMB 59051
350 Fifth Avenue, 59th Floor
New York, New York 10118

Published in the United Kingdom
Crabtree Publishing
Maritime House
Basin Road North, Hove
BN41 1WR

Published in Australia
Crabtree Publishing
3 Charles Street
Coburg North
VIC, 3058

CONTENTS

Chapter 1
Food Today and Tomorrow   4

Chapter 2
What Makes an Argument?   8

Chapter 3
Should There Be an Age Restriction on Buying
  Junk Food?   20

Chapter 4
Should Genetically Modified Foods Be Banned?   28

Chapter 5
Should Schools Cut Break Times to Provide
  Cooking Classes?   36

Bibliography   44
Glossary   46
Learning More   47
Index and About the Author   48

CHAPTER 1
FOOD TODAY AND TOMORROW

Food is the fuel we need to live. Food production is an immense, worldwide **industry**. It includes growing crops, raising livestock, fishing, transporting food to market, and **manufacturing**, advertising, and selling food products.

The Importance of Good Food

In some parts of the **developing world**, food is often in short supply. **Drought**, floods, and war can lead to food shortages and **famines**, when large numbers of people are in danger of starvation. **Malnutrition** leads to delays in children's growth and development, disease, and even death.

In contrast, in the developed world, there is an increasing problem with **obesity**. This is a condition in which a person's body weight is more than 20 percent higher than what is healthy, based on their age, body type, and **gender**. More people are becoming overweight and obese from eating too much junk food with a high sugar or fat content. Heart problems and diseases such as **diabetes** are also linked to this kind of diet. Food intake needs to be balanced with regular exercise. Many people have **sedentary** jobs, which means they sit for most of the day. Often, they do not exercise enough to stay healthy. This means that the health care system has to treat people for medical conditions that could be prevented by healthy eating and activity.

Governments and Food

In most countries, there are many government regulations about food safety, covering issues such as hygiene and pollutants. Governments also encourage healthy eating and exercise by trying to educate people about them. In some countries, such as the United Kingdom (UK), taxes on unhealthy foods such as sugary sodas

A healthy diet is especially important for young people. Eating healthy food helps their bodies develop as they grow.

The food industry involves growing crops and raising animals, as well as processing, checking, packaging, and transporting food to stores.

are being considered. There is also talk of placing age restrictions on buying junk food. This is meant to discourage children and teenagers from eating unhealthy foods and becoming overweight. Around the world, governments and education boards have created rules that make sure students get exercise for a certain number of minutes per day. There is now some debate about whether some of this time could be spent in classes that teach children about healthy eating instead.

Food Additives and Modifications

The food industry uses many **preservatives** to keep food products fresh. In some foods, chemicals are used to improve the taste, smell, texture, or color. In a number of countries, animals that are bred for food are given growth **hormones** to make them bigger. Many people are concerned that these practices might be harming the health of people who eat the food.

The food industry also produces **genetically modified (GM)** foods. These are foods that are produced from plants that have had their genes altered. Genes are the parts of **DNA** that contain the instructions for how they look and grow. These genetically modified **organisms**, or living things, are referred to as GMOs.

Genetically modified crops can be more resistant to drought, frost, diseases, and pests. Some GM crops **yield**, or produce, extra-large harvests and stay fresh for longer periods of time. GM crops could help to increase food production in parts of the world where shortages are common. However, there are concerns about whether GM food is safe to eat. There is also concern that the production of GM crops damages **ecosystems** by altering the natural balance between insects and plants.

FOOD TODAY AND TOMORROW

Hot Topics?

Many of us feel passionately about the food that we eat and the ways we choose to stay healthy. This means that there are many strong, and sometimes opposing, opinions about food and its effects. For example, many people argue that governments should place a tax on sugary drinks. Others claim that GM foods are harmful and believe that such foods should be banned. People debate which foods are healthy and which are harmful. Some, for example, argue that junk food is causing so many health problems that there will be a crisis in health care in the future.

Most food products have lists of their ingredients on the label. This means that people can see what the food contains and decide whether or not to buy the product.

Arguing About Food

You probably often hear, read, and see friends, family, scientists, and newscasters presenting their opinions in arguments about food and healthy eating. You need to be able to work through the arguments to decide which ones are **credible**—and which are not. That way, you can start to form your own opinions about food and how it affects you.

In this book, we'll take a look at the arguments about food and the food industry. We'll look at the features of an argument, what makes a strong argument, and how to decide if you agree with it or not. Let's start by taking a look at the argument on the opposite page, about whether everyone should become **vegetarians**. A vegetarian is a person who does not eat meat and, sometimes, other animal products.

Do You Agree?

"Should everyone be vegetarian?"

EVERYONE SHOULD BECOME A VEGETARIAN.

Killing animals for food is cruel. Every year, more than 58 billion farm animals are killed. Many of them, such as cows and pigs, are kept in confined spaces. Young animals are taken from their mothers before this separation would naturally happen.

Humans do not need to eat meat. In fact, vegetables and fruits provide our bodies with many of the **nutrients** we need. While **protein** is found in meat, we can also get protein from eggs, beans, and some vegetables. Meat contains **saturated fats**, which can lead to heart disease. A 2016 study by the American Osteopathic Association found that people eating a long-term vegetarian diet had an increased **life expectancy** of 3.6 years. Vegetarians have an 11 percent smaller chance of developing cancer, according to a 2014 study by Oxford University, UK.

EVERYONE SHOULD NOT BECOME A VEGETARIAN.

Vegetarians are at risk of missing out on some essential nutrients. Omega-3 fats found in oily fish help the brain work. Nuts and dairy products do not contain as much protein as meat and fish. Vegetarianism also does not make people healthy on its own. They still need to exercise and avoid fatty and sugary foods. A 2014 study of 15,000 people at the Institute of Social Medicine and **Epidemiology** (the study of disease) in Graz, Austria, found that vegetarians had poorer health and needed medical treatment more often.

If people are worried about cruel treatment of animals, they can buy meat that is free-range or is "**certified humane**." This means that the animals have been well looked after and kept in fields rather than pens. It also means they have been slaughtered in a way that did not cause them any unnecessary pain. If all humans were vegetarian and no meat was produced, this would mean many job losses in the meat industry.

After reading the arguments above, decide which side you agree with. How did you make your choice? Did you rely on personal experience? Does the way the arguments are presented influence your decision?

CHAPTER 2
WHAT MAKES AN ARGUMENT?

Informal discussions with our friends can be a good way to practice forming effective arguments. Through conversations, you can get in the habit of backing up your opinions with evidence.

An argument is a set of reasons based on **logic**. It shows that a person's belief or position on an issue is **valid**, or correct. An argument can be used to try to change another person's point of view, or to persuade them to accept a new point of view. Arguments can also be used to draw support or promote action for a cause.

Why Argue?

You read, hear, and see arguments every day. You might see two people arguing about the healthiest ingredients to use in a recipe. Each person states their ideas, gives their reasons, and, if the argument is strong, supports their reasons with **evidence** to try to persuade the other person that their ideas are best.

Arguments can be used in different ways. Sometimes an argument can help people learn about an issue. It might explain one or both sides to an issue so people can make an informed decision about what they believe. For example, an argument might explain why GM crops are a benefit to farmers in the developing world.

Other arguments are persuasive. They are meant to gather support for a cause or to get others to agree with certain beliefs. A persuasive argument might convince more restaurants to include the **calorie** counts for meals on their menus. Persuasive arguments try to influence the way you think about something, or change your mind about an issue.

Other arguments are used to solve problems and make decisions. For example, members of a school community might present arguments about whether to give money to promote healthy eating or to exercise programs at the school. When both sides of an argument are heard, people can come to a decision about how they should act on an issue.

Arguments are not always serious. Sometimes people present arguments to learn about and discuss opposing ideas.

Prove Your Point

An argument is made up of a number of **claims**, or statements about why a viewpoint is correct. To prove that your argument is correct, you need to give evidence that supports your claims, or proves that they are true. When you are evaluating an argument, it is up to you to decide whether the person making the argument has supported their claims with evidence.

*There are many sources of evidence, such as facts and **statistics**. Many of these sources can be found by conducting research online.*

WHAT MAKES AN ARGUMENT?

Building an Argument

A good argument needs to be built carefully. It has the following features, or parts:

Core Argument

The **core argument** is your position, or where you stand, on the topic or issue. Your core argument states what you believe to be true. It is the main point that you will try to prove in your argument. Arguments state the core argument in their introduction. An example of a core argument is:

> *Preservatives, or substances that keep food from rotting, and chemicals in our food should be more strictly **regulated**.*

Claims

Your claims are the statements that support your core argument. An example of a claim is:

> *Preservatives and chemicals in our food may cause people health problems.*

Reasons

Reasons are details that support your claim. They explain why you have made that specific claim. An example of a reason is:

> *Sugar and artificial sweeteners can cause health problems including obesity, dental cavities, and diabetes, and increase the amount of fat in the blood. Some preservatives may cause damage to the liver and **nervous system**.*

Evidence

A good argument supports its reasons with evidence. Evidence might be a quotation from an interview with someone who is considered to be an expert on the topic. It could be statistics from a study of people affected by an issue, or facts about the topic. Without evidence, an argument cannot be proven to be true.

Hot dogs contain a number of chemicals and preservatives to keep the meat fresh and to maintain its color.

> Not everything you read is credible, so you need to assess whether the evidence is valid. You can do this by asking questions such as:
> - Who is the author of the source of information? Are they knowledgeable on the subject?
> - Where did the information come from? Is it a respected organization?
> - When was the source written? If it was several years ago, the information might be out-of-date.
> - Do other sources have similar information? If not, you may need to evaluate whether this source is credible.

This is an example of credible evidence. It comes from a doctor who is an expert in the field.

> *Sodium nitrate is a preservative used to stop meat from becoming rotten. According to **cardiologist** Martha Grogan, sodium nitrate increases the risk of heart disease. This is because it can cause blood vessels to harden and narrow. **Nitrates** can also affect the way the body processes sugar, and according to Grogan, this increases a person's risk of diabetes.*

Counterclaims

To make an argument even stronger, a person needs to take note of the possible **counterclaims** against their argument. Counterclaims support the opposite viewpoint to the argument. After making claims and giving reasons and evidence, a person making an argument should write down the strongest counterclaim against their argument. They should then respond to the counterclaim, using evidence, to prove why their argument is stronger. This is an example of a counterclaim:

> *Preservatives in our food make it safer. According to the Centers for Disease Control and Prevention (CDC), every year, at least one in six Americans suffers from food poisoning. Preservatives stop the spread of the bugs that cause illness. "Removing preservatives compromises food safety, and there is no good scientific reason to avoid them," says Robert Brackett, director of the Institute for Food Safety and Health. However, cardiologist Martha Grogan says that the common preservative sodium nitrate can increase the risk of heart disease by causing blood vessels to harden and narrow.*

Conclusion

Your conclusion should restate your main argument and reasons. An example of a conclusion is:

> *Although more scientific testing is still being done, the results of tests so far shows that some of the preservatives and chemicals in our food might cause health problems. There is enough evidence for us to believe that some **additives** need to be more strictly regulated.*

Researching the topic will help you gather evidence and enable you to form a stronger argument.

WHAT MAKES AN ARGUMENT?

Evaluating Arguments

You can evaluate an argument by looking at its features. Examine the argument below about placing a tax on sugary sodas. A tax is money taken off income, or added onto product sales (such as soda), and paid to the government. Does the argument include all of the features it needs to be a strong argument? When you have finished reading, decide if you think this argument is strong.

CORE ARGUMENT

Sodas that contain a large amount of sugar should be taxed because taxing could discourage people from buying them, resulting in better health and health care savings.

CLAIM

Sodas with high sugar content increase the risk of many health problems.

REASON

Beverages that contain a large amount of added sugar, such as sodas and energy drinks, can increase the risk of diabetes and obesity. The sugar in sodas can also cause tooth decay, or the breaking down of a tooth's surface.

EVIDENCE

According to the World Health Organization (WHO), 500 million people around the world were classed as obese in 2015, including 42 million children under five years old. According to studies by Public Health England (PHE) in 2015, sodas make up 29 percent of the daily sugar intake for people in the UK age 11 to 18. In a 2017 review by the *European Journal of Obesity* about studies into the issue, 93 percent of the studies found that sugary sodas are linked to children and adults gaining weight. "We are now in a place where we can say there is enough evidence to move on this, and we encourage countries to implement effective tax on sugar-sweetened beverages to prevent obesity," says Temo Waqanivalu, of the Department of Noncommunicable Diseases and Health Promotion at the WHO.

A 12-ounce (355 ml) can of soda may contain as much as 10 teaspoons of sugar.

Money raised from sugar taxes could be put into sports programs. This would promote a healthier lifestyle.

CLAIM

Taxing sugary sodas would help improve the health of people and save money spent on health care.

REASON

If sugary sodas became more expensive, some people would choose cheaper beverages. Their health would then improve, and the health care system would have fewer people with obesity-related illnesses to care for in the future. The taxes raised from sodas could also be spent on health care for those currently suffering from obesity and diabetes, or on healthy living programs.

EVIDENCE

In 2012, France placed a tax on beverages with added sugar. This led to a 3.3 percent fall in sales. In 2014, Mexico placed a sugar tax on sodas, which led to a 6 percent decrease in sales. In the future, these countries may see an improvement in people's health, resulting in savings in health care costs.

COUNTERCLAIM

In the United States, the drinking of soda has been declining since the beginning of the century. As a result, some people say that a sugar tax is not needed. Many towns already ban sugary beverages from schools, limit them in vending machines, and teach children about healthy eating. However, evidence indicates that sugar taxes work to stop more people from drinking a lot of soda and would bring even greater falls in soft drink sales. It is very important that we ensure the health care system is not overwhelmed by preventable illnesses.

CONCLUSION

It is clear that the high sugar content in sodas is linked to obesity, diabetes, and other health problems. If these beverages cost more money, people would drink less of them. People would live longer and healthier lives, and health care costs would be reduced. In addition, the extra money gained in taxes could be spent on community sports leagues.

WHAT MAKES AN ARGUMENT?

Making a Great Argument

A core argument, claims, reasons, evidence, counterclaims, and a conclusion are the important parts of an argument. But there are also other elements that make a great argument.

Who Is Your Audience?

Knowing who your **audience** is will help you target your argument. You can base your argument on details about your audience, such as their age, gender, or background.

An audience made up of people who are interested in the topic must be approached differently from those who are not familiar with it. For example, a school chef may have strong opinions about healthy food for children. People of different ages have different perspectives. Younger people who have grown up eating fast food may have a different view about it from someone who ate mostly home-cooked meals as a child. A person's lifestyle, their job, and where they live, may also affect how they feel. When you make an argument, it is important to keep your audience in mind, and ensure that your claims and evidence will relate to them.

Introductions Count

Before clearly introducing your core argument, your introduction should get the reader interested in the topic. For example, an argument in favor of a sugar tax could begin with the following introduction:

> *Did you know that when a sugar tax was proposed in the UK in 2016, it was expected to raise $680 million? This money could be spent on health care for those with diseases related to consuming too much sugar. Worldwide soft drink sales are around $870 billion, so a tax would raise a lot of money.*

Clincher Conclusions

The conclusion is as important as your introduction. It restates your core argument and claims. Your conclusion should end with a **clincher**. This is a statement that strengthens your argument by capturing the reader's attention right at the end, so that they are more likely to consider all your points and agree with you.

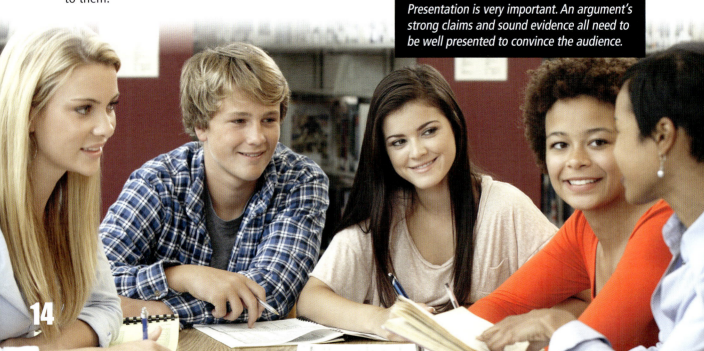

Presentation is very important. An argument's strong claims and sound evidence all need to be well presented to convince the audience.

In the argument about the benefits of a sugar tax, your clincher could state:

> Given the links between health problems such as obesity and diabetes, and beverages with high sugar content, as well as evidence that a tax does reduce consumption, a sugar tax on soft drinks would be very beneficial for public health now and in the future. People would become healthier, and there would be less pressure on the health care system since fewer people with preventable illnesses would need treatment. If children lead healthier lives, they will grow into healthy adults.

A clincher can also be a quote or a question that makes the reader think, such as:

> Shouldn't we be using sugar taxes to not only improve health, but also to generate money to improve health care, so that more people get the help they need?

> Health care systems are already overburdened, and costs are rising. Encouraging people to eat healthy food would reduce some of the stress on the health care system.

Choose Your Words

The words you use and how you use them will help persuade people to see and appreciate your point of view. Words can appeal to someone's emotions and strengthen the evidence that you present. For example, referring to sources of facts and statistics will back up your claims. Mentioning qualified experts and quoting from them will also make people more likely to believe you. Words can appeal to people's emotions by emphasizing things they care about. In the sugar tax argument, words might **emphasize**, or stress, the damage that sugary sodas cause to the health of children around the world.

WHAT MAKES AN ARGUMENT?

Powerful Words

How effective an argument is depends on the types of words used. **Rhetoric** is the art of using language effectively when writing or speaking. Rhetoric is usually used in persuasive speaking or writing.

Persuasive Trio

There are three types of rhetoric: logos, pathos, and ethos.

Logos: Logos uses logic and reason to prove a point. Logos is an ancient Greek word from which we get the word "logic." Logos often uses facts and statistics. A logical argument backed up with solid facts will help others consider your position, even if they do not agree with it. Here is an example of logos:

> Monosodium glutamate (MSG) is in many processed foods and soups. It is used to enhance flavor. Some people are sensitive to MSG and experience nausea, breathing problems, and high **blood pressure**. In 2016, researchers in Food and Chemical Toxicology found that MSG damages the body's cells.

Pathos: An argument based on pathos appeals to the audience's emotions with personal stories. Stating that some people developed high blood pressure from MSG does not relate to audience members who do not know what high blood pressure is. However, a story about a person living with high blood pressure not only appeals to the audience's emotions, but also provides an example to show why the statistic is important. Pathos should be used only to support your claim. It should not be used to confuse or frighten people in order to win an argument. A good example of pathos is:

> Andy ate a lot of processed food for most of his life. He was diagnosed with high blood pressure at age 40. Five years later, he had a **stroke** caused by his high blood pressure. He did not have full use of his right hand and arm for three months. He also had to have speech therapy to help with slurred speech.

Ethos: Ethos is the way that a person can establish that they can be trusted. The language used shows the person's qualifications and knowledge about an issue. The person speaking usually tells the audience about their qualifications, or uses reliable quotes from experts. The speaker can also respect the opposing view and present it correctly to the audience to establish trust. An example of ethos is:

> As a cardiologist at Bellevue Hospital in Manhattan, New York, I have treated hundreds of patients whose lives have been ended prematurely thanks to heart disease caused by an unhealthy diet.

MSG is commonly found in some Asian foods, to enhance their flavor.

In 2017, the world population of cattle was 998.3 million. Around 63 percent of cattle on Earth are found in India, Brazil, and China.

LOOKING AT LANGUAGE

Read the following statement. Can you identify the rhetoric the author has used?

Did you know that becoming vegetarian could benefit the environment? The livestock industry takes up almost 30 percent of the land on Earth, and causes 18 percent of all **greenhouse gas** emissions. Cows release the greenhouse gas methane. In fact, livestock produce more greenhouse gasses than cars on the roads, which produce about 14 percent of emissions. Around 80 percent of farmland in the United States is used to raise animals or grow food for them. Instead, this farmland could be used to produce food to feed people who are hungry. Don't you think humans should all become vegetarians for the good of Earth and its inhabitants?

Which types of rhetoric does the statement use to appeal to the audience? What words or phrases make you think so?

17

Where Do You Stand?

Read these two arguments about whether governments should limit the amount of **imported** foods that grocery stores can sell. Keep in mind the features of an argument and the power of language. Which argument do you feel is stronger? Why?

Governments Should Limit the Imported Foods on Sale.

Local or national producers should get preference over food producers from other countries because local food is healthier, better for the environment, and benefits local **economies** more than imported foods. Limiting the amount of imported food helps protect the local economy, community, and jobs, because people buy from local producers. In 2006, a study by **market research** firm Ipsos found that 70 percent of Canadians thought that buying local foods helped their local economy and family farmers.

Local foods travel shorter distances than imported foods. This means that they are fresher when they reach the grocery store.

Local food is fresher and healthier. It usually does not contain preservatives because it is eaten locally and soon after being harvested. Some people also believe that local food tastes better. "When we eat local produce, the taste is so much more superior over produce that we're bringing in from overseas," says Canadian registered dietician Karlene Karst. Eating local foods is better for the environment, too. In the United States, the average food item travels between 1,200 and 2,480 miles (1,931 and 3,991 km) before it is bought. **Fossil fuels** such as gas are used to transport food in airplanes and trucks, which creates pollution.

Some people argue that limiting imported foods might not be a good idea, because locally produced food is often more expensive. However, a 2016 survey from LoyaltyOne found that 61 percent of Canadians would pay up to 30 percent more for local food.

Based on the fact that local food is often fresher and healthier, governments should limit the amount of imported food in stores. This would also reduce pollution. In addition, buying food from local producers is important because it supports farmers and boosts the local economy.

Governments Should Not Limit the Imported Foods on Sale.

Governments should import foods for sale in grocery stores because it gives shoppers more variety and maintains **trade** relationships, or the buying and selling of goods, with other countries. People like to have a choice in what groceries they buy. Many foods cannot be grown locally. For example, communities in cold climates cannot grow fruits such as mangoes. Allowing imports gives shoppers more variety to choose from. "We've had so many great advances in shipping and logistics and the ability to get things moved from point A to point B very quickly, so that we can enjoy the benefits of having fresh things year-round," says Susan Abel, vice president of safety and compliance at Food and Consumer Products of Canada (FCPC).

Importing foods from other countries keeps international trade going. Countries depend on trading goods with one another. Limiting the amount of imported foods could lead to other countries restricting imports. The United States is the world's largest food **exporter**. In 2014, U.S. food exports were worth $149 billion. Canada is the fifth-largest food exporter in the world. The U.S. and Canada rely on trade to export their products. If those exports stopped, many people would lose their jobs.

Some people claim that reducing the amount of imported food would benefit local food producers and local economies. However, local economies are linked with the national—and worldwide—economy. If international trade in food were damaged, there would be widespread job losses across North America.

Based on the variety that imported foods bring to grocery stores, and the need to maintain international trade, governments should not limit the amount of imported food in grocery stores.

Farmers markets are popular places for people to buy their food. However, usually only items grown locally can be bought there.

CHAPTER 3
SHOULD THERE BE AN AGE RESTRICTION ON BUYING JUNK FOOD?

Junk food such as sodas, chocolate bars, and chips are sold in grocery stores, gas stations, and vending machines. Fast-food restaurants in most cities and towns sell junk food to customers looking for a quick meal. Many people like to eat junk food, but it has many negative health effects—especially on children and youth. Some people think young people should not be allowed to buy it.

Junk food is food that is high in calories but low in nutrients. Junk food contains large amounts of sugar and fat, but not many vitamins, **fiber**, minerals, and protein. Types of junk food include: french fries, chocolate, cookies, ice cream, doughnuts, and sugary sodas.

Problems with Junk Food

Lack of activity and too much junk food, as well as large portion sizes at meals, is causing many children to gain weight and become obese. It is estimated that one in three children and teenagers in the United States is overweight or obese. When young people pick up bad eating habits, they are more likely to continue eating poorly when they become adults. Some **nutritionists** and health educators suggest setting an age restriction on the buying of junk food to keep children from developing these bad habits. They argue that this would also prevent them from developing serious health problems related to obesity when they are older. They propose that youth under the age of 18 should not be able to buy junk food.

There are already age limits on buying some harmful products in North America and many other countries. For example, people under 21 years of age are not allowed to buy alcohol in the United States. In Canada, the age restriction is 18 or 19, depending on territory or province. Across North America, the minimum age for buying tobacco ranges from 14 to 21. Today's teens are well educated about the health risks of these products, just as they know the health risks of junk food. Even so, the government has decided that young people need to be protected from using substances such as alcohol and tobacco until they are old enough to take responsibility for themselves.

Young people enjoy junk food, but it can lead to them developing unhealthy eating habits early in life. This can cause health issues when they are older.

Making Good Decisions

Some people argue that everyone should decide for themselves which foods they eat. They think that we already have too many regulations telling us what to do. Some people argue that, rather than banning young people from buying junk food, more money should be put into education about the dangers of a poor diet, or into programs that support healthy living, such as sports. Others think that putting higher taxes on unhealthy foods might be a better way of reducing the amount of junk food that everyone eats.

A ban might be hard to implement because not everyone agrees on which foods are classified as junk food. Some foods considered to be junk foods can be eaten in **moderation** without harming our health. For example, pizza has nutrients in the tomato sauce and cheese, and vegetables can be used as toppings. Pizza can also be made with whole wheat dough, making it a relatively healthy option to eat occasionally.

There are many types of junk food. They are all designed to taste good so that people will want to eat them, but they contain little nutritional value.

So, what are the arguments for and against an age restriction on buying junk food?

JUNK FOOD TODAY

Here are some interesting statistics about junk food:

- Every day, 50 million Americans eat at a fast-food restaurant.
- 45 percent of Canadians buy at least one junk food product each day.
- A 2017 national poll by C. S. Mott Children's Hospital, in Ann Arbor, Michigan, found that 97 percent of parents think that childhood eating habits shape children's health throughout their life, but only 13 percent rated their child's diet as "very healthy."

There Should Be an Age Restriction on Buying Junk Food.

Junk food is bad for the health of children and youth, so they should not be allowed to buy it. It is important for children to eat healthy food while they are growing up, so that their bodies continue to develop properly. Foods with high sugar content, such as sodas and chocolate bars, affect energy levels in children as they can lead to sharp rises and falls in blood sugar. Sugar can also cause problems with concentration and focus. If a child has consumed a large amount of sugar, hormones in the brain are released that interfere with memory, so they find it hard to focus in class, sit quietly at their desk, or remember all that they have been taught. Junk food does not provide the human body with enough nutrients, such as protein and carbohydrates, to create long-term energy. This leads to irritability and tiredness just an hour or two after eating the food.

A 2013 study by the *Journal of the American Academy of Child and Adolescent Psychiatry* concluded that a diet high in junk food caused emotional and behavioral problems in children. In 2008, the *Journal of School Health* stated that students who ate low-quality food did worse than their **peers** on **standardized tests**. When children and teenagers eat too much junk food, these eating habits often continue when they are older. Obesity in children can lead to them developing high blood pressure, diabetes, and high **cholesterol** levels as adults. A 2004 study by the journal *Pediatrics* found that a diet including large amounts of junk food increased the risk of obesity. In the early 1970s, the obesity rate for children was between 4 and 6 percent. This had risen to between 10 and 20 percent by 2008.

Children and young people need to be protected from the constant encouragement to eat junk food that comes from advertising and the easy availability of junk food. Around 33 percent of Americans are obese, including 19 percent of children and teenagers. A 2004 study published in the medical journal *The Lancet* found that, over time, eating more than twice a week at fast-food restaurants is linked to people gaining more weight than if they ate fast food only occasionally. In 2009, researchers at the University of California, Berkeley, found that people living near a fast-food restaurant had a 5.2 percent greater

Many children eat junk food regularly. Combined with little exercise, eating junk food can lead to obesity and poor health.

Junk food is popular with adults as well as children. Many people in North America and around the world enjoy visiting fast-food restaurants.

risk of becoming obese than those who did not. Since 1970, the number of fast-food restaurants has doubled, and there are now around 300,000 across the U.S. In 2011 and 2012, data from the National Health and Nutrition Examination Survey (NHANES) found that children and teenagers in the U.S. got an average of 12.4 percent of their daily calories from fast food. Professor Ian Caterson of the World Obesity Federation explains, "Fast-food advertising continues to really influence food choices and what is eaten."

Some people argue that junk food is only harmful when it is eaten too often and in high quantities. Instead, children should be taught to make good choices about the food they buy and eat. However, placing age restrictions on products gives a further level of protection for children against the harmful effects of junk food. Placing restrictions would work well to stop children from buying, and therefore eating, junk food. In the United States, California, New Jersey, Oregon, Hawaii, and Maine have changed the age at which people can buy cigarettes to 21. In 2015, the Institute of Medicine published a report concluding that raising the minimum tobacco sales age to 21 nationwide would reduce smoking by 25 percent among 15- to-17-year-olds and by 15 percent among 18- to-20-year-olds.

Due to the dangers of eating junk food and the links between it and obesity, there should be an age restriction on the buying of junk food to protect people's health. If young people do not get into the habit of eating junk food while they are growing up, they are less likely to eat it as adults and more likely to lead healthier lives.

There Should Not Be an Age Restriction on Buying Junk Food.

An age restriction on buying junk food does not guarantee that children and youth will not eat it. Parents, older siblings, or friends can buy it for them. As a result, an age restriction on under-18s buying junk food would be meaningless.

Junk food is fine in moderation, and people should decide for themselves whether to eat it. Although junk food is not healthy, it can be enjoyed sometimes as long as it is accompanied by plenty of exercise and other, healthier food. Junk food becomes a problem for your health only if eaten in large amounts on a regular basis. Treats eaten every now and then, such as a cookie or ice cream on an outing, make us happy. The health risks of eating fast food and other junk foods are also well known. People should be allowed to make up their own minds about what to eat. The Academy of Nutrition and Dietetics (AND) supports the idea of eating certain foods in moderation. That means it is acceptable to eat something that is not good for you as long as you eat only a small amount and not very often.

"It is the position of the Academy of Nutrition and Dietetics that the total diet or overall pattern of food eaten is the most important focus of healthy eating. All foods can fit within this pattern if consumed in moderation with appropriate portion size and combined with physical activity."

An occasional sweet treat does not do any harm, especially when combined with a healthy lifestyle and regular exercise.

Some people maintain that eating any junk food is a bad idea, because it can cause bad habits and health problems. But the eating habits of children often come from the food their parents feed them. Therefore, if parents are educated about healthy eating habits, an age restriction is not necessary. A 2017 survey by the C. S. Mott Children's Hospital in Michigan found that 97 percent of parents in the U.S. believe a child's eating habits while growing up will affect what they eat as an adult. However, education for parents is needed. The same study found just 17 percent of parents think they are providing their children with a healthy diet. Around half said they did not know which foods were healthy. Parents may also need help in learning how to encourage their children to eat healthy foods when they are offered: Around 60 percent of parents said their children did not like healthy food and resisted eating it.

Having an age restriction for buying junk food would not work because children could get others to buy it for them. A better option would be to educate parents and children about healthy eating and how junk food can be enjoyed in moderation, as part of a healthy diet and lifestyle.

For younger children, it is the responsibility of parents to ensure that children have a healthy diet.

SHOULD THERE BE AN AGE RESTRICTION ON BUYING JUNK FOOD?

STATE YOUR CASE

When it comes to any issue, you have to look at arguments on both sides before you decide where you stand. Remember the features of effective arguments when you consider the arguments for and against an age restriction on buying junk food. Which side's argument do you think is stronger? Why do you think so? Give reasons for your answers. Use the "In Summary: For and Against" list to help you figure out your decision, and state your own case.

IN SUMMARY: FOR AND AGAINST

For an Age Restriction on Buying Junk Food

Junk food is bad for children's health.

- Foods with high sugar content affect energy levels and concentration in children.
- Eating junk food has led to an increase in obesity in many countries.
- Obesity in children can lead to high blood pressure, diabetes, and high cholesterol levels in later life.

Junk food is advertised and easily accessible, so children should be protected from making poor choices and buying it.

- Fast-food places are everywhere, while advertisements for junk food are frequently on television.
- People living near a fast-food restaurant have a 5.2 percent greater risk of being obese.
- Children and teenagers in the U.S. get an average of 12.4 percent of their daily calories from fast food.

Sweet and fatty foods may taste great, but can be very damaging to our health. Developing poor eating habits as children can lead to bad eating habits as adults.

Against an Age Restriction on Buying Junk Food

Age restrictions for children buying junk food would not keep them from eating it.

- Parents, older siblings, and friends could buy junk food for underage children.
- Parents need to be educated about healthy shopping and eating to change their children's eating habits. A 2017 study found that just 17 percent of parents felt they were feeding their children healthy diets. Therefore, the problem is with parents who feed their children junk food, rather than children buying it themselves. A restriction is unnecessary.

Junk food is fine in moderation and people should decide for themselves whether to eat it.

- Small amounts of junk food are not that harmful if people get plenty of regular exercise and eat mostly healthy food.
- Treats eaten every now and then make us happy and help us enjoy life more.
- There is a lot of information available about the effects of different foods. People should be allowed to make their own choices based on this information.

Children's eating habits come from the foods that their parents feed them from a young age. A ban on junk food for children is not needed because parents often feed them junk food anyway.

CHAPTER 4
SHOULD GENETICALLY MODIFIED FOODS BE BANNED?

The first GM food was the Flavr Savr tomato, which was first sold in the United States in 1994. Today, GM foods are grown in more than 20 different countries. More than 50 percent of the world's GM foods are grown in the United States, while Canada grows around 6 percent. However, how good are GM foods for us?

GM foods are produced from plants that have been altered by modifying their DNA (deoxyribonucleic acid). DNA is found in the cells of almost all living things. It contains the instructional information that genes use to make sure living things grow a certain way.

Living things can be modified by changing their DNA. For example, if you want to have green strawberries, you could take DNA from a green apple and add it to strawberry DNA. Some things can also be taken away from a plant's DNA, too. For example, a fruit that produces large seeds could be modified to produce smaller ones.

What Are GM Foods?

Fruits, vegetables, soybeans, and corn are the most common GM foods in grocery stores. Corn is used in many different products, including corn syrup, which is widely added to food products as a sweetener. GM grain is often used in animal feed. Some farm animals, such as cows, chickens, pigs, and goats, are also genetically modified, but no GM animals are currently farmed for their milk or meat.

GM plants are often **adapted**, or changed, so they can better survive bad weather conditions, such as drought or frost. Others are altered so they are less affected by pests and diseases. Modified fruits and vegetables ripen more quickly. They also stay ripe for longer, allowing them to be transported farther for sale. These traits are useful for all farmers. They can be especially useful in the developing world, where many people are in need of crops that can withstand different weather. Many people hope that GM crops can prevent famines and improve people's lives.

Some genetic modifications help plants grow better, and some create qualities that will make people want to buy them.

28

Safety Questions

There are concerns about whether eating GM foods may affect our health, and what effects GM plants could have on the environment. Some people think GM foods should be banned. Others think more tests need to be done on GM foods to see what long-term effects they may have.

In the United States and Canada, GM food is not labeled as GM, which means people do not always know they are buying it or eating it. However, GM ingredients such as oils or sweeteners are in more than 80 percent of North American packaged goods. Around 90 percent of the soy, cotton, **canola**, and field corn grown in the United States is GM. However, other countries have restrictions on GM crops. In the European Union (EU), the sale of GM foods is limited because they have not been proven to be safe to eat.

So, what are the arguments for and against banning genetically modified foods?

This protest took place in Toronto, Canada. The protesters believe that GM foods should always be labeled as "GM" on their packaging.

GM FOOD BY NUMBERS

Here are some interesting statistics about GM food:

- At least 90 percent of U.S. agricultural crops have been genetically engineered in some way.
- Around 30,000 square miles (77,700 sq km) of GM canola was seeded in Canada in 2016.
- More than 230,000 square miles (595,697 sq km) of GM corn and soybeans are grown in the United States every year.
- 64 countries have laws that require GM foods to be labeled.

GM Foods Should Not Be Banned.

GM foods should not be banned because they are safe to eat, can be superior to non-GM food, and can even save lives. GM foods are perfectly safe to eat. In fact, they can even be more nutritious than non-GM food. GM foods have already been sold and eaten for more than 20 years. In that time, there have been no safety issues for people or animals. In fact, humans have been altering plants for thousands of years. For example, people have bred different kinds of wheat to create stronger versions of the plant. GM fruits, vegetables, and other plants keep fresh for longer than normal plants. This makes it easier to transport them to more places and over longer distances, so that more people can eat them. GM foods can have their taste improved, making them sweeter or spicier. GM foods can also be engineered to be more nutritious than regular foods. There have been 130 research projects by the European Commission into the safety of GM crops, none of which have found any dangers. Nutrients can also be added to GM foods. Rice does not normally have **vitamin A**, but it is added to rice crops in developing countries where people suffer from malnutrition. This vitamin is important for the body's growth and development.

GM foods can save lives. They can help fight food shortages and starvation in the developing world. GM plants are designed to resist extreme weather, diseases, and pests. This means that farmers will always have a good crop, reducing the possibility of crop failure and the hunger it could lead to. GM crops can be grown in areas with poor soil that were not previously suitable for farming. Farmers also spend less time and money on **pesticides** to kill insect pests and on farmworkers to monitor the crops. David Zilberman, an agricultural and environmental economist at the University of California, Berkeley, says that the use of GM crops "has raised the output of corn, cotton, and soy by 20 to 30 percent, allowing some people to survive that would not have without it. If it were more widely adopted around the world, the price [of food] would go lower, and fewer people would die of hunger."

These GM plums, called C5, contain an extra gene that makes them highly resistant to plum pox virus. This disease makes the fruit taste too bitter to eat.

The United Nations Food and Agriculture Organization says that by 2050, the world will have to grow 70 percent more food to feed everyone on the planet. GM crops will be a great help because they can be grown in dry or salty soil, in high or low temperatures, resist insects and diseases, and produce higher yields.

While there are advantages to GM foods, some people worry that altering plants could be dangerous. They think that dangers to our health or effects on the environment may not show up for years, by which time it will be too late. However, the fact that GM plants are altered to be insect and disease repellant means that farmers need to use fewer pesticides on their crops—both of which can have harmful effects on humans, too. David Zilberman at University of California, Berkeley, says that the use of GM crops "has increased farmer safety by allowing them to use less pesticide." This also protects the environment from dangerous chemicals. Pesticides from farms can get into rivers and lakes, resulting in catastrophic damage to the ecosystem and the death of fish and other aquatic life.

GM foods should be allowed because they are more resistant to pests and diseases, they last longer so that more people can enjoy eating them, they are safe to eat, and can be even more nutritious. They could also ensure than people in developing countries have enough nutritious food to eat, which is one of the greatest challenges the world currently faces.

GM foods have the potential to help supply food in places where famine is common, such as Bangladesh.

GM Foods Should Be Banned.

GM foods should be banned because they could be harmful to humans and the environment. GM foods have not existed for long. We have no way of knowing if they could cause health problems in the future. If GM foods cause disease in humans, the problem might not show up for decades. Genetic modification may add **allergens** to foods that were not there before, which can cause serious health problems for people with allergies. More than 40 countries, including Australia, Japan, and some members of the EU, restrict or do not allow the sale of GM foods. This is because they are not yet proven to be safe. More people have food allergies today than in the past. The CDC found that in the United States, food allergies in children under 18 years old increased from 3.4 percent between 1997 and 1999 to 5.1 percent between 2009 and 2011. A study at Brown University, Rhode Island, found that GM foods are probably responsible for the increased number of allergic reactions in some people.

GM foods may be harmful to the environment. Farmers spray their fields with **herbicides** to keep weeds away. GM crops have been modified to be resistant to herbicides. That means that farmers can spray a lot more herbicide to kill weeds, without it harming the crops. The problem is that this has led to weeds themselves becoming resistant to some herbicides, too. The weeds become resistant after getting used to the chemical, as a result of being sprayed so much. Research in 2016 by University of Virginia economist Federico Ciliberto found that 28 percent more herbicides are now being used on GM soybeans. "Evidence suggests that weeds are becoming more resistant, and farmers are having to use additional chemicals, and more of them," says Ciliberto. A 90 percent reduction in the population of the monarch butterfly in the United States is believed to have been caused by weed killer used on GM crops.

Not all foods containing GM ingredients are labeled. If these foods are supposed to be safe, some people think that they should know exactly what they are eating.

*Monarch butterflies are **native** to the northern and central United States and Canada. They have been threatened by the increased use of herbicides on fields with GM crops.*

Supporters of GM crops say that modified foods have to meet the same safety standards and undergo the same tests as foods grown from regular seeds. Yet, even if GM foods are tested, the rules about how they are sold are too relaxed. It is not required in the United States or Canada for GM ingredients to be labeled. This means that people do not really know what they are buying and eating. Even if there is no clear evidence as yet that GM foods are harmful, people have a right to know so that they can decide whether or not to buy GM products. In parts of Europe and Asia, there is mandatory labeling of GM foods. GM foods should be banned, at least until a fair system is in place that informs people what GM ingredients are in foods.

GM foods should be banned because the risks to health and the environment are still not clear. Until more tests are done to ensure GM foods are safe, they should not be on our supermarket shelves.

STATE YOUR CASE

When it comes to any issue, you have to look at arguments on both sides before you decide where you stand. Remember the features of effective arguments when you consider the arguments for and against genetically modified foods. Which argument do you think is the strongest? Why do you think that one side is more powerful than the other? Give reasons for your answers. Use the "In Summary: For and Against" list to help you figure out your decision, and state your own case.

IN SUMMARY: FOR AND AGAINST

For GM Foods

GM foods are safe to eat, last longer than normal foods, and can be more nutritious.

- GM foods have already been eaten for more than 20 years, during which time there have been no safety issues for people or animals.
- There have been 130 research projects by the European Commission into the safety of GM crops, none of which has found any dangers.
- GM produce stays fresh for longer than regular produce.
- GM foods can have their taste improved, making them sweeter or spicier.
- GM foods can be engineered to be more nutritious than regular foods, such as by adding vitamin A.

Genetically modified foods can save lives.

- GM foods can help fight food shortages and starvation in the developing world.
- GM plants are designed to resist extreme weather, diseases, and pests.
- GM crops can be grown in areas with poor soil that were not previously farmed.
- Farmers spend less time and money on pesticides and on farmworkers to monitor GM crops.

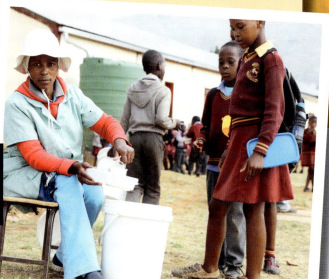

When crops fail in the developing world, people can be at risk of starvation. GM crops may be one way to avoid this.

Against GM Foods

GM foods may not be safe and could cause health problems.

- If GM foods cause disease in humans, the problems might not show up for decades.
- More than 40 countries, including Australia, Japan, and some members of the EU, restrict or do not allow the sale of GM foods because they are not yet proven to be safe.
- Genetic modification may add allergens to foods. According to a study by Brown University, GM foods are probably responsible for an increased number of allergic reactions.

GM foods may be harmful to the environment.

- GM crops are leading to increased use of weed-killing herbicides, which can damage insect populations, such as monarch butterflies.
- GM farmers can spray as much herbicide as they want on their GM crops, which may be encouraging the growth of superweeds that are resistant to them.
- Research in 2016 by the University of Virginia found that 28 percent more herbicides are being used on GM soybeans.

*Herbicides threaten bees. Bees are very important and **pollinate** many different plants, which would not be able to survive without them.*

CHAPTER 5
SHOULD SCHOOLS CUT BREAK TIMES TO PROVIDE COOKING CLASSES?

Today, many people are so used to eating prepared and packaged meals or fast food that they are unsure how to cook healthy meals for themselves. Children growing up today do not have many opportunities to learn about nutrition and cooking healthy meals when they are at school. Some people feel that this needs to change.

Cooking at School

In the United States, cooking is taught in some high schools but not all of them. It is not usually a required course for students. Many people think that this is a great failing in the school system. There have been suggestions that cooking classes should be set up in schools to teach children about food preparation. Classes would educate students about which foods are nutritious and which cooking methods are healthiest. The hope is that if children are educated on healthy cooking, they will eat less packaged meals and junk food, which are high in unhealthy fats, salt, and sugar.

However, where can these cooking classes fit into the school schedule? Teachers must give students the skills they will need to join the workforce. Subjects such as language arts, social studies, math, and science are essential, and a certain number of hours dedicated to them have to be included in the school **curriculum**. In some cases, a second language, computer classes, or physical education are also required as a part of the weekly lessons.

When students work together in cooking classes, they can build important skills such as teamwork and communication.

Getting plenty of exercise and fresh air is just as important as maintaining a healthy diet. Children need a break from the classroom during the day.

The Right Recipe for Success

One way to come up with the time needed to provide cooking classes to students is to reduce the amount of time children spend on breaks.

However, while cooking classes might be a very good idea, children also still need to take breaks during the day. Their focus, concentration, and desire to learn might suffer if they do not have a chance to relax between classes. Some parents might also object to their children having less free time while they are at school.

It is accepted that people need to eat more healthy food. It is also true that people who never learn to cook can prepare only very basic meals, which are likely to make use of packaged foods containing additives, preservatives, salt, sugar, and fat. Teaching children cooking skills at an early age is a good idea. However, fitting it into the school day is a major challenge.

So, what are the arguments for schools cutting break times to provide cooking classes?

Schools Should Cut Break Times to Provide Cooking Classes.

It is a good idea to cut school break times to provide cooking classes because of the benefits to students' health and the skills they can develop. Cooking classes will encourage young people to make healthy food choices. If students learn about healthy eating when they are young, they are more likely to become healthier adults. People who do not know how to cook healthy meals are more likely to eat packaged foods or fast foods, which have low nutritional value. This might lead to obesity or other health issues. Even if teaching cooking takes some time away from breaks at school, it is worthwhile. Rob Rees, chairman of the School Food Trust in the UK, argues that all children should have the chance to learn to cook.

"Fundamentally, being able to cook is a life skill which helps children grow into healthier adults, and that's why our evidence to the national curriculum review calls for practical cooking to be compulsory for all children." In 2017, research in the *Journal of the Academy of Nutrition and Dietetics* stated that children who cooked were more likely to try a variety of things to eat.

Cooking classes will provide students with valuable social skills, and other skills such as cooperation, communication, responsibility, and **self-esteem**. The **social interaction** students have at break times can also happen in a cooking class. Students learn cooperation and

In cooking classes, people learn how healthy, fresh ingredients can be combined to create different flavors.

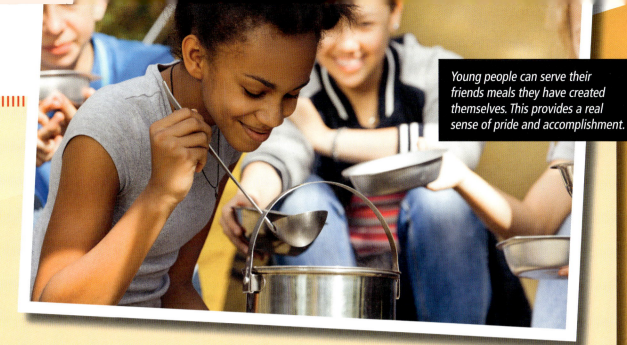

Young people can serve their friends meals they have created themselves. This provides a real sense of pride and accomplishment.

communication skills as they work together and learn in a group setting. In 2011, the Colorado State University Department of Food Science and Human Nutrition conducted research into the impact cooking classes have on students. Participants in cooking classes said that they had opportunities to enhance their social skills. "This study documents the importance of including cooking in the school curriculum, as it is a practical mechanism to promote health, and social and educational skills to better prepare students for adulthood," said Dr. Leslie Cunningham-Sabo, Assistant Professor at Colorado State University. Students who take part in cooking classes also learn responsibility, as they are required to follow rules about kitchen safety and cleanliness, and take a role in their healthy eating practices. Creating dishes that are healthy and delicious boosts students' self-esteem. Students also have the opportunity to practice math skills such as counting, weighing, measuring, and tracking time.

Some people argue that cooking classes in school are not enough to make children develop healthy eating habits. They say it is not worth cutting valuable break times to provide classes that are not proven to make a difference in students' habits at home. However, evidence shows that cooking classes can ignite an interest in cooking, which can translate into life outside of school. "People find personal satisfaction in cooking, or come to view the experience as a way to tap into their creativity," says Dr. David Eisenberg of the Department of Nutrition at the Harvard T. H. Chan School of Public Health.

Schools should cut break times to provide classes that teach students how to cook healthy meals, because if children know how to cook, they are more likely to make healthy eating choices. Children also learn valuable life and social skills during cooking classes that will help them at school and prepare them for their adult life.

Schools Should Not Cut Break Times to Provide Cooking Classes.

It is not a good idea to cut break times to add cooking classes into schools because break times are too important and because academic classes are more valuable than cooking classes. Children need break times to remain healthy and able to learn to the best of their ability. Break times allow students to recharge and be ready to learn. Break times are also very important to keep children active and help to fight obesity. During break times, children also learn how to get along with each other, follow rules, keep safe, and even how to communicate. In 2009, the Albert Einstein College of Medicine, New York, conducted a study of 11,000 children age eight and nine. The study found that children behaved better in class if they had at least 15 minutes of recess each day. According to developmental pediatrician Romina Barros, this was most likely because they could rest their brains before going back to learning. A 2013 study by the Robert Wood Johnson Foundation found 42 percent of children in the U.S. get most of their daily exercise at recess. This was more than the exercise they got in after-school programs or physical education sessions. Olga Jarrett, professor of Early Childhood and Elementary Education in the College of Education & Human Development at Georgia State University, says that recess is better for children than gym class. "With recess, children have choices and can organize their own games, figure out what's fair, and learn a lot of social behavior that they don't learn in PE (physical education)."

Education is very important, but time away from the classroom helps students maintain good mental health and focus.

Classes in STEM topics are more important to a student's future education and career prospects than cooking and nutrition classes.

If children are going to have extra classes, they should be in academic subjects because they are more valuable than cooking classes. During the school day, it is vital that children learn the skills they will need when they join the workforce. If break times are cut to provide extra classes, these should be in subjects such as math or science. Math and science are becoming more important every year as we use more technology in our lives and work. Science, technology, engineering, and mathematics are together called **STEM**. According to the U.S. Department of Commerce, STEM jobs are growing at 17 percent per year. Other types of jobs are only growing at 9.8 percent. People working in STEM jobs have higher salaries than those in other fields. For example, in 2014, the U.S. Department of Education reported that STEM majors had annual salaries of around $65,000, which was $15,500 more than non-STEM majors.

Some people claim that learning to cook is just as important a skill as math or science, as every child's health depends on the food they eat. However, today's children and teenagers spend much of their time in front of screens, which is also damaging to their health. According to 2015 research by Childwise in the UK, children age five to 16 have around 6.5 hours of screen time per day. With this in mind, it is very important that young people have break times at school to get enough exercise. The 2008 publication *Physical Activity Guidelines for Americans* says that children age 6 to 17 should spend at least one hour on physical activity every day. Teaching them about healthy cooking and eating won't matter if they don't exercise as well.

Schools should not cut break times to provide cooking classes because children need breaks so that they get enough exercise. They also need to have a rest every now and then, so that they can better absorb the information from their teachers. If schools cut break times to provide classes, they should be in important subjects that will help students get jobs when they graduate from high school.

STATE YOUR CASE

When it comes to any issue, you have to look at arguments on both sides before you decide where you stand. Remember the features of effective arguments when you consider the arguments about schools cutting break times to provide cooking classes. Which argument do you think is the most convincing? Why do you think that one is better than the other? Give reasons for your answers. Use the "In Summary: For and Against" list to help you figure out your decision, and state your own case.

IN SUMMARY: FOR AND AGAINST

For Schools Cutting Break Times to Provide Cooking Classes

Cooking classes will encourage young people to make healthy food choices.

- Teaching cooking educates students about making smarter food choices.
- If students learn about healthy eating when they are young, they are more likely to become healthier adults.
- Eating healthier meals greatly improves a person's health by reducing their risk of developing diseases such as obesity and diabetes.

Cooking classes will provide young people with valuable social and other skills.

- The social interaction students have at recess can also happen in cooking class.
- Students learn to cooperate as they work together in a group setting.
- Students learn how to follow rules about safety with kitchen equipment.
- Cooking provides a fun way for students to practice and learn basic math skills.
- Creating a healthy and delicious dish that students can take home to their family can help improve their self-esteem.

Cooking classes give students the tools they need to develop healthy eating habits.

Against Schools Cutting Break Times to Provide Cooking Classes

Students need full break times each day to remain healthy.

- Students need breaks so that they can focus in the classroom. Research shows that they behave better in class with at least 15 minutes of recess each day.
- Students need to spend time outside and get exercise to remain healthy. A 2013 study by the Robert Wood Johnson Foundation found that 42 percent of U.S. children get most of their daily exercise at recess.
- Children learn social skills in the playground.

If children are going to have extra classes, they should be in academic subjects.

- During the school day, it is vital that children learn the skills they will need when they join the workforce.
- If break times are cut for extra classes, these should be in subjects such as math.
- According to the U.S. Department of Commerce, STEM jobs are growing at 17 percent per year, while other types of jobs are only growing at 9.8 percent.

Students of all ages get vital exercise during recess. They also learn social skills such as communication, tolerance, and cooperation.

BIBLIOGRAPHY

Food Today and Tomorrow

Barrington, Vanessa. "The 10 Biggest Problems With the Global Food System." Ecosalon, October 5, 2010. http://ecosalon.com/the-10-biggest-issues-with-the-global-food-system

"Becoming a Vegetarian." Harvard Health Publications, December 4, 2017. www.health.harvard.edu/staying-healthy/becoming-a-vegetarian

"Childhood Obesity Facts." Centers for Disease Control and Prevention, January 29, 2018. www.cdc.gov/healthyschools/obesity/facts.htm

"Facts and Figures on Childhood Obesity." World Health Organization, October 13, 2017. www.who.int/end-childhood-obesity/facts/en

Heneghan, Carolyn. "9 Food and Beverage Experts Identify the Industry's Biggest Challenges in 2017." Food Dive, January 4, 2017. www.fooddive.com/news/food-and-beverage-biggest-challenges-2017/433164

Lewis, Rachel. "The Immediate Effect Fast Food Has on Children." *The National*, May 13, 2013. www.thenational.ae/lifestyle/family/the-immediate-effect-fast-food-has-on-children-1.317147

Lockhart, Emily. "7 Pros and Cons of Switching to a Vegetarian Diet." Active Beat. www.activebeat.com/diet-nutrition/7-pros-and-cons-of-switching-to-a-vegetarian-diet

Martinac, Paula. "Disadvantages of a Vegetarian Diet." LiveStrong, October 3, 2017. www.livestrong.com/article/85540-disadvantages-vegetarian-diet

"Nutrition Tips for Kids." Family Doctor, July 20, 2017. https://familydoctor.org/nutrition-tips-for-kids

"Proven Advantages and Disadvantages of Vegetarianism." Healthy Futures. https://healthyfuturesva.com/proven-advantages-and-disadvantages-of-vegetarianism

Segal, Jeanne Ph.D., and Robinson, Lawrence. "Healthy Food for Kids." Help Guide, March 2018. www.helpguide.org/articles/healthy-eating/healthy-food-for-kids.htm

"Statistics." Childhood Obesity Foundation, April 2015. http://childhoodobesityfoundation.ca/what-is-childhood-obesity/statistics

What Makes an Argument?

Baum, Kathryn Blaze. "Soft Drinks, Hard Decisions: What Canada Is Doing Amid the Global Sugar Tax Debate." *The Globe and Mail*, November 12, 2017. www.theglobeandmail.com/news/national/sugar-tax-debate-canada-soda-childhood-obesity/article36591805

Bruso, Jessica. "Advantages and Disadvantages of Artificial Food Preservatives." LiveStrong, October 3, 2017. www.livestrong.com/article/533477-advantages-and-disadvantages-of-artificial-food-preservatives

"Constructing an Argument." Massey University, February 8, 2018. http://owll.massey.ac.nz/study-skills/constructing-an-argument.php

Dlugan, Andrew. "What Is Logos and Why Is It Critical for Speakers?" Six Minutes, August 15, 2010. http://sixminutes.dlugan.com/logos-definition

"Examples of Ethos, Logos, and Pathos." Your Dictionary. http://examples.yourdictionary.com/examples-of-ethos-logos-and-pathos.html

"Facts on Animal Farming and the Environment." One Green Planet, November 21, 2012. https://www.onegreenplanet.org/animalsandnature/facts-on-animal-farming-and-the-environment

Girard, Patrick. "Good and Bad Arguments." Future Learn, University of Auckland. www.futurelearn.com/courses/logical-and-critical-thinking/0/steps/9153

Gonchar, Michael. "200 Prompts for Argumentative Writing." *The New York Times*, February 4, 2014. https://learning.blogs.nytimes.com/2014/02/04/200-prompts-for-argumentative-writing

Karp, David. "Most of America's Food Is Now Imported. Is That a Bad Thing?" *The New York Times*, March 13, 2018. www.nytimes.com/2018/03/13/dining/fruit-vegetables-imports.html

"Local vs. Imported Fruit: What Tastes Better and How to Tell the Difference." *CTV News*, August 29, 2016. https://bc.ctvnews.ca/local-vs-imported-fruit-what-tastes-better-and-how-to-tell-the-difference-1.3049705

Logan, Nick. "Is There an Argument Against 'Buy Local'? You Bet." *Global News*, June 9, 2015. https://globalnews.ca/news/2042704/is-there-an-argument-against-buy-local-you-bet

Marron, Donald. "Should Governments Tax Unhealthy Food and Drinks?" *Forbes*, December 14, 2015. www.forbes.com/sites/beltway/2015/12/14/should-governments-tax-unhealthy-foods-and-drinks/#2cd547f026fb

Nardelli, Alberto and Arnett, George. "Will a Sugar Tax Actually Work?" *The Guardian*, March 16, 2016. www.theguardian.com/news/datablog/2016/mar/16/will-a-sugar-tax-actually-work-budget

Nebehay, Stephanie. "Tax Sugary Drinks to Fight Obesity, WHO Urges Governments." Reuters, October 11, 2016. www.reuters.com/article/us-health-sugar/tax-sugary-drinks-to-fight-obesity-who-urges-governments-idUSKCN12B0ZB

"New Evidence Links Sugary Drinks and Obesity." *Psychology Today*, January 30, 2018. www.psychologytoday.com/us/blog/evidence-based-living/201801/new-evidence-links-sugary-drinks-and-obesity

"Overview of Food Ingredients, Additives, and Colors." U.S. Food and Drug Administration, 2010. www.fda.gov/Food/IngredientsPackagingLabeling/FoodAdditivesIngredients/ucm094211.htm

Ranzi, Karen. "Nutrients in Local Produce Versus Imported Produce." Super Healthy Children, July 6, 2016. https://superhealthychildren.com/nutrients-in-local-produce-versus-imported-produce

Schulten, Katherine. "10 Ways to Teach Argument-Writing with *The New York Times*." *The New York Times*, October 5, 2017. www.nytimes.com/2017/10/05/learning/lesson-plans/10-ways-to-teach-argument-writing-with-the-new-york-times.html

"Should There Be a Tax on Soda and Other Sugary Drinks?" *The Wall Street Journal*, July 12, 2015. www.wsj.com/articles/should-there-be-a-tax-on-soda-and-other-sugary-drinks-1436757039

Weida, Stacey, and Stolley, Karl. "Using Rhetorical Devices for Persuasion." Purdue Online Writing Lab, March 11, 2013. https://owl.english.purdue.edu/owl/resource/588/04

Zelman, Kathleen. "The Vital Role of Food Preservatives." *Food & Nutrition*, February 27, 2017. https://foodandnutrition.org/march-april-2017/vital-role-food-preservatives

Should There Be an Age Restriction on Buying Junk Food?

"A Portrait of Canadian Youth." Statistics Canada, February 7, 2018. www.statcan.gc.ca/pub/11-631-x/11-631-x2018001-eng.htm

"Are Food Manufacturers to Blame for Obesity?" Fitday. www.fitday.com/fitness-articles/nutrition/beyond-willpower-are-food-manufacturers-to-blame-for-obesity.html

Bambenek, Cadence. "Facts About Today's Teens' Technology, Social Media Use, and Sex." *Business Insider*, June 29, 2016. www.businessinsider.com/teen-technology-use-2016-6

Boseley, Sarah. "Junk Food Shortening Lives of Children Worldwide, Data Shows." *The Guardian*, October 7, 2016. www.theguardian.com/society/2016/oct/07/junk-food-shortening-lives-children-obesity-diabetes-data

Casselbury, Kelsey. "Negative Effect of Junk Food on Kids." LiveStrong, August 14, 2017. www.livestrong.com/article/456624-negative-effects-of-junk-food-on-kids

Conrad, Dr. Brent. "Media Statistics—Children's Use Of TV, Internet, and Video Games." TechAddiction. www.techaddiction.ca/media-statistics.html

"Fast Food Nutrition: Junk Food's Affect on Your Body." Fitday. www.fitday.com/fitness-articles/nutrition/healthy-eating/fast-food-nutrition-junk-foods-effect-on-your-body.html

Harris, Jennifer, and Samantha Graff. U.S. National Library of Medicine, National Institute of Health, February 2012. "Protecting Young People from Junk Food Advertising." www.ncbi.nlm.nih.gov/pmc/articles/PMC3483979

Kazi, Safeeyah. "Western Culture Is to Blame for Rising Childhood Obesity in Developing Countries." *The Independent*, October 15, 2017. www.independent.co.uk/voices/obesity-uk-usa-developing-countries-western-culture-chains-a8002026.html

Ketler, Alanna. "Shocking Fast-Food Statistics and How You Can Begin Eating Better." Collective Evolution, 2017. www.collective-evolution.com/2017/02/27/shocking-fast-food-statistics-how-you-can-begin-to-eat-better

Lehman, Shereen. "When Eating Something Bad Is Actually Good." Very Well Fit, June 15, 2018. www.verywellfit.com/moderation-when-eating-something-bad-is-actually-good-2505928

Magee, Elaine. "Junk Food Facts." Web MD. www.webmd.com/diet/features/junk-food-facts#1

Miller, Christa. "Is Junk Food OK in Moderation?" LiveStrong, October 3, 2017. www.livestrong.com/article/479487-is-junk-food-ok-in-moderation

"Protecting Children from the Harmful Effects of Food and Drink Marketing." World Health Organization, September 2014. www.who.int/features/2014/uk-food-drink-marketing/en

Renee, Janet. "Statistics of Health Risks for Eating Fast Food." LiveStrong, July 18, 2017. www.livestrong.com/article/383621-statistics-of-health-risks-from-eating-fast-food

"The Effects of Sugar on a Child's Academic Performance." Learning Liftoff, June 25, 2015. www.learningliftoff.com/the-effects-of-sugar-on-a-childs-academic-performance

"The Impact of Food Advertising on Childhood Obesity." American Psychological Association. www.apa.org/topics/kids-media/food.aspx

Welch, Ashley. "Is Junk Food to Blame for the Obesity Epidemic." *CBS News*, November 5, 2015. www.cbsnews.com/news/junk-food-obesity-epidemic

Should Genetically Modified Foods Be Banned?

Fagin, Dan. "Why We Should Accept GMO Labels." *Scientific American*. October 24, 2013. www.scientificamerican.com/article/why-we-science-should-accept-gmo-labelings

Freedman, David. "The Truth About Genetically Modified Food." *Scientific American*, September 1, 2013. www.scientificamerican.com/article/the-truth-about-genetically-modified-food

"Frequently Asked Questions on Genetically Modified Foods." World Health Organization, May 2014. www.who.int/foodsafety/areas_work/food-technology/faq-genetically-modified-food/en

"Genetically Modified Foods." *The Canadian Encyclopaedia*. www.thecanadianencyclopedia.ca/en/article/genetically-modified-foods

"Genetically Modified (GM) Crops in Canada." Statista. www.statista.com/topics/3013/genetically-modified-gm-crops-in-canada

Kelly, Margie. "Top 7 Genetically Modified Crops." *Huffington Post*, December 30, 2012. www.huffingtonpost.com/margie-kelly/genetically-modified-food_b_2039455.html

Should Schools Cut Break Times to Provide Cooking Classes?

Copp, Phoebe. "Top 5 Reasons for Teaching Nutrition Education in Your Classroom." Dairy Council of California. www.healthyeating.org/Schools/Tips-Trends/Article-Viewer/Article/521/Top-5-Reasons-to-Teach-Nutrition-Education-in-Your-Classroom

Crampton, Lina. "Pros and Cons of Making Food and Nutrition Compulsory Subjects." Owl Nation, June 28, 2017. https://owlcation.com/academia/Pros-and-Cons-of-Making-Food-and-Nutrition-Compulsory-Subjects

Dent, Grace. "Teaching Children to Cook at School Is a Recipe for Self-Respect." *The Independent*, May 4, 2015. www.independent.co.uk/voices/comment/teaching-children-to-cook-at-school-is-a-recipe-for-self-respect-10224159.html

Ipatenco, Sara. "Nutrition in the High School Curriculum." LiveStrong, October 3, 2017. https://www.livestrong.com/article/433592-nutrition-in-the-high-school-curriculum

Jacobs, Peter. "Science and Math Majors Earn the Most Money after Graduation." *Business Insider*, July 9, 2014. www.businessinsider.com/stem-majors-earn-a-lot-more-money-after-graduation-2014-7

McFarland, Mary Anne. "Cooking with Kids in Schools: Why It Is Important." Extension, February 9, 2017. http://articles.extension.org/pages/73371/cooking-with-kids-in-schools:-why-it-is-important

"Physical Activity Facts." Centers for Disease Control and Prevention. www.cdc.gov/healthyschools/physicalactivity/facts.htm

"Recess Helps Kids Learn Better in School." American Heart Association, May 8, 2018. https://news.heart.org/recess-helps-kids-learn-better-in-school

"The Impact of Cooking Education Programs on Children." Curious Chef, March 3, 2015. http://curiouschef.com/healthy-eating/blog/the-impact-of-cooking-education-programs-on-children

"Why Is STEM Education So Important?" Engineering for Kids, February 2, 2016. www.engineeringforkids.com/about/news/2016/february/why-is-stem-education-so-important

GLOSSARY

Please note: Some **boldfaced** words are defined where they appear in the text.

additives Substances added to something, usually to improve or preserve it

allergens Substances that cause an allergic reaction

audience Spectators, listeners, or readers

blood pressure The amount of force the pumping blood puts on the walls of the veins and arteries as it moves through the body

calorie A unit of energy used to measure the amount of energy provided by food

canola A crop from which cooking oil is made

cardiologist A medical doctor who specializes in the functioning of the heart and circulatory system

cholesterol A substance containing a lot of fat found in the body tissue and blood of all animals

credible Believable or convincing

curriculum The subjects that teachers have to teach students at school

developing world A term often used by the United Nations and other organizations to describe countries where things such as average income, the strength of the economy, infrastructure such as roads, and poverty, education, and health care are lower or less available in comparison to "developed" countries, such as those in Europe and North America

diabetes A disease that results in too much sugar in the blood

DNA An acronym for deoxyribonucleic acid; DNA is present in the cells of nearly all living things and carries instructional information

drought A long period of low rainfall, leading to a shortage of water

economies The prosperity and earnings of places, such as countries or towns

ecosystems Communities of organisms and their natural environments

evidence Anything, such as data or statistics, that proves or disproves something

exporter A business or country that sells goods to another country

famines Extreme food shortages

fiber Dietary material that helps you digest other food

fossil fuels Resources such as oil, natural gas, and coal that formed over millions of years from dead plants and animals

gender The state of being male or female

greenhouse gas Gas found in Earth's atmosphere that traps heat in a process known as the greenhouse effect

herbicides Substances used to kill weeds and other unwanted vegetation

hormones Substances produced by the body that make parts of the body do specific things

imported Brought into a country from a foreign source

industry Specific types of businesses that make goods or provide services

life expectancy How long someone or something is expected to live

logic A system of thinking and figuring out ideas

malnutrition A lack of proper nutrition caused by not having enough to eat

manufacturing Making goods by hand or by machines or both

market research Collecting and studying information about what people want, need, and buy

moderation Not too much or too little

native Describes something that lives and grows naturally in a particular place

nervous system The brain and the network of nerves that carry messages around the body

nitrates Chemical compounds containing nitrogen and oxygen. Nitrates help plants grow.

nutrients Substances that nourish a living thing and keep it healthy

nutritionists People who are experts in nutrition

peers People who are equal in ability, qualifications, age, background, or social status

pesticides Substances used to kill insects or other living creatures that harm animals or plants

pollinate Take pollen from one plant or part of a plant to another, so that new plant seeds can be produced

preservatives Substances used to keep foods fresher for longer

protein A nutrient found in food that is a necessary part of a person's diet

regulated Controlled or supervised using rules and regulations

saturated fats Fats considered to be unhealthy, usually found in animal products

sedentary Describes a relatively inactive lifestyle

self-esteem Confidence in one's own worth and abilities

social interaction Engaging in activities with other people in person

standardized tests Tests that are taken nationally to measure students' learning

statistics Facts involving numbers or data

stroke A sudden loss of brain function caused by a blockage or rupture of a blood vessel in the brain

vitamin A The vitamin important for normal vision, tissue growth, and healthy skin

yield To give results; the amount of crop harvested per area of land

LEARNING MORE

Find out more about the arguments surrounding food issues around the world.

Books

Are You What You Eat? A Guide to What's on Your Plate and Why. DK Children, 2015.

Quinlan, Julia J., and Adam Furgang. *The Truth Behind Snack Foods* (From Factory to Table: What You're Really Eating). Rosen Central, 2018.

Rissman, Rebecca. *Genetically Modified Food* (Food Matters). Core Library, 2015.

Steele, Philip. *Analyzing the Food Supply Chain: Asking Questions, Evaluating Evidence, and Designing Solutions* (Analyzing Environmental Change). Cavendish Square, 2018.

Websites

Read more on issues in the food industry and its future:
www.ft.com/reports/future-food-industry

Learn more about writing and evaluating arguments and counterclaims:
www.icivics.org/products/drafting-board

From buying choices to healthy eating tips, find out about the importance of healthy foods at school on this website:
https://kidshealth.org/en/kids/school-lunches.html

Find out more about genetically modified foods in the United States:
https://ohioline.osu.edu/factsheet/HYG-5058

Find out more about genetically modified foods in Canada:
www.unlockfood.ca/en/Articles/Food-technology/Understanding-Genetically-Modified-Foods.aspx

INDEX

Academy of Nutrition and Dietetics (AND) 24
additives 11, 37
age restrictions 5, 23
alcohol and tobacco 20
allergens 32, 35

bees 35
break times 36, 37, 38, 39, 40, 41, 42, 43

Centers for Disease Control and Prevention (CDC) 11
certified humane 7
Childwise 41
claims 9, 10, 11, 14, 15
clincher 14, 15
conclusion 11, 14
cooking classes 36, 37, 38, 39, 40, 41, 42
core argument 10, 14
counterclaims 11, 14
curriculum 36, 38, 39

developing world 4, 8, 28, 30, 34
diabetes 4, 10, 11, 12, 13, 15, 22, 26, 42
DNA 5, 28

eating habits 20, 21, 22, 25, 26, 27, 39, 42
environment 17, 18, 29, 31, 32, 33, 35
ethos 16
evidence 8, 9, 10, 11, 12, 13, 14, 15, 33, 38, 39
exercise 4, 5, 7, 9, 22, 24, 27, 37, 40, 41, 43

famines 4, 28
farmers 8, 18, 28, 30, 31, 32, 35
farmers markets 19
fast food 14, 22, 23, 24, 26, 36
Flavr Savr tomato 28
Food and Consumer Products of Canada (FCPC) 19
food industry 5, 6

gender 4, 14
GM foods 6, 28, 29, 30, 31, 32, 33, 34, 35
greenhouse gas emissions 17
grocery stores 18, 19, 20, 28

health care 4, 6, 12, 13, 14, 15
health risks 20, 24
healthy eating 4, 5, 6, 9, 13, 24, 25, 38, 39, 42

junk food 4, 5, 6, 20, 21, 22, 23, 24, 25, 26, 27, 36

life expectancy 7
logic 8, 16
logos 16

monarch butterflies 33
MSG 16

nervous system 10
nitrates 11
nutrients 7, 20, 21, 22

obesity 4, 10, 12, 13, 15, 20, 22, 23, 26, 38, 40, 42

packaged meals 36
pathos 16
pesticides 30, 31, 34
preservatives 5, 10, 11, 18, 37
Public Health England (PHE) 12

recess 40, 42, 43
rhetoric 16, 17

saturated fats 7
self-esteem 38, 39, 42
sports 13, 21
standardized tests 22
statistics 9, 10, 15, 16, 21, 29
STEM jobs 41, 43
sugar tax 13, 14, 15

University of California, Berkeley 22, 30, 31

vegetarian 6, 7, 17

World Health Organization (WHO) 12
World Obesity Federation 23

ABOUT THE AUTHOR

Simon Rose is an author of 15 novels and more than 100 nonfiction books. He offers programs for schools, covering the writing process, editing and revision, where ideas come from, character development, historical fiction, story structure, and the publishing world. He is an instructor for adults and offers online workshops and courses. Simon also provides services for writers, including manuscript evaluation, editing, and coaching, plus copywriting services for the business community.